CREATE AND CELEBRATE

The
Easter Tree

Text copyright © 2022 Lion Hudson IP Limited
This edition copyright © 2022 Lion Hudson IP Limited
Illustrations by Artful Doodlers
Text by Deborah Lock

Published by **Lion Children's Books**
Part of the SPCK Group,
SPCK, 36 Causton Street, London SW1P 4ST
www.lionhudson.com

ISBN 978 0 7459 7935 9

First edition 2022

Acknowledgments

Scripture quotations on p. 44 are taken from the Good News Bible © 1994 published by the Bible Societies/ HarperCollins Publishers Ltd UK, Good News Bible© American Bible Society 1966, 1971, 1976, 1992. Used with permission.

Scripture quotations on p.16 and p. 47 are taken from The Holy Bible, International Children's Bible® Copyright© 1986, 1988, 1999, 2015 by Tommy Nelson™, a division of Thomas Nelson. Used by permission.

A catalogue record for this book is available from the British Library

Printed and bound in China, November 2021, LH54

CREATE AND CELEBRATE

The Easter Tree

A Lent Activity and Story Book

Text by Deborah Lock

LION
CHILDREN'S

Introduction

If you look out of the window during Lent, you will see that there are beginning to be more leaves and buds on the trees each day. Spring is coming, and they are getting ready to look their best. Easter is coming too. Between now and then, there are 40 days of Lent (or 46 if you count the Sundays). Lent gives us an opportunity to get ready for Easter as we think about Jesus and all he means to us.

Using this book, you can take a bare tree or branch and fill it with wonderful things in time for Easter. Each day, there will be a little bit of Jesus' story to read, and a decoration to make for your Easter tree. The decorations have all sorts of symbols on them, and by the time you have finished, your tree will be far from bare.

Trees are not just for looking at, though. You can sit under them, or play around them, or even climb in them if you are careful. Each day, there is something to do as well. This might be a promise to keep, a message to send, or just something to think about.

When I was little, my dad would sometimes stop me on a walk through the forest to look at a tree stump. Together we would look at the rings and count them to know how old the tree had been. "Every tree tells a story," my dad would say. This Easter Tree wants to tell a story too, and you can help it to do just that. Let's get started!

Richard Littledale

Contents

Set–up Instructions

For the Easter Tree, use a tree branch with lots of twigs and set it into a pot of sand or stones. If your branch already has new leaves and blossoms, add some water to the pot. If not, attach some small green paper leaves and pink tissue paper balls for blossom. You may also wish to paint the twig and branches white.

Use this QR code to access a download of the templates.

To make the
Easter Tree decorations

You need:
Shiny metallic card,
white card, glue, strips of ribbon,
hole punch, marker pens

Optional:
glitter, sequins,
felt or wool material

1   Cut 40 oval shapes, at least 12 cm in length out of the metallic card.

2   For each day, use the symbol provided as a template to trace onto white card and cut out, OR use the QR code on the page opposite to download the templates to cut out.

3   Decorate the symbol, using pens and other decorative bits, then glue onto a metallic oval.

4   Make a hole at the top, using the hole punch, and thread a strip of ribbon through it.

5   Tie the ends of the ribbon to make a loop for hanging onto your Easter Tree.

GLUE

Tip: You could laminate the decorations before making the hole to make them last longer.

In the wilderness

Symbol: desert rock

Jesus went into the wilderness to prepare for the work God had planned for him. For forty days and forty nights, Jesus spent time with God alone and without food. He was exhausted and the devil came to tempt Jesus away from God. To test Jesus, the devil asked Jesus to use his divine power to turn rocks into bread, and promised him wealth and power, and an easy way to save the world. Jesus remained strong, replying with words of God, who he wanted to glorify and serve.

Matthew 4, Luke 4

Like a lizard basking on a desert rock, spend some time reflecting and preparing to resist temptations and to focus on God and the needs of others.

A miraculous catch

Symbol: fish in a net

On the shores of Lake Galilee, people crowded around Jesus to hear him talk about God. He asked a fisherman, Simon Peter, if he could talk to the people from his boat. After he had finished talking, Jesus said to Peter and his brother Andrew, "Let's go fishing." They had been fishing all night and had not caught anything, but they did as Jesus said. When they put down the nets, they caught so many fish that they called to some fishermen nearby, James and John, to help them. They were amazed, for both boats were nearly sinking under the weight of all the fish. "Come, follow me," Jesus said, and they did.

Luke 5

Like the huge catch of fish, think about something BIG and amazing that has happened in the world. Thank God for this miraculous work.

The wedding

Symbol: water-jars

Jesus, his mother, and his friends were invited to a wedding in the town of Cana. Soon, the wine ran out for the guests. Jesus told the servants to fill the six large stone water-jars used for washing and then pour a drink for the steward in charge of the banquet. The steward was impressed. The water had become the best wine. Only the servants knew that Jesus had done this.

John 2

Think about the water you have used today. Are there ways that you could perhaps use less so there is more to share?

Blessings

Symbol: hands giving and receiving

On the mountains around Lake Galilee, Jesus sat down to talk to his followers. He taught that the kingdom of God belonged to people who are humble, peaceful, and eager to do the right thing. Jesus promised that those who mourn or are attacked for what they believe in will receive comfort and see God. They are blessed and happy because of all that they will receive as children of God. These eight blessings are known as the Beatitudes.

Matthew 5

Find out about a country where people are attacked for following Jesus, and how they can be given help and hope.
www.opendoors.uk.org

Salt and light

Symbol: sprinkling salt

Jesus used images to show how those who followed his teachings would have an amazing impact on the lives of others. His followers would be like salt and light. Salt can change food either for the good to prevent rotting or the bad to no longer taste good. Jesus wanted his followers to change the world for good. They were to be a light, glorifying God with their good deeds and showing others God's goodness.

Matthew 5

Like sprinkling salt, think of a way that you can make a difference to someone's life today with a good action.

"Stand up"

Symbol: stretcher

There was a man who could not walk. His friends wanted to bring him to Jesus, but the house was crowded. So the friends lowered the man on his mat down through the roof. Jesus showed his power to forgive and heal. "Stand up and walk," he said to the man. Suddenly, the man stood up, picked up his mat and went home, praising God. Everyone was amazed.

Matthew 9, Mark 2, Luke 5

The stretcher symbol is a reminder to think about those who need help. Do you have a friend that needs help?

The two builders

Symbol: sandcastle

Jesus explained that someone who follows him is like a builder who builds a strong house on rock with deep foundations. This follower listens to his words and acts on them. But someone who listens, but does not act, is like a builder who builds a house on sand. A strong house stands firm through any storms in life, but a weak house falls to ruin.

Matthew 7, Luke 6

Make a promise to keep, rather than letting it wash away like a sandcastle.

Symbol: door

Jesus said to his followers that God was their Father in heaven, who wants to give an abundance of good things to his children. He told them how they should talk and listen to God through prayer. God wants people to ask for help, to seek and find God by praying, and to knock on God's door continuously, eager to be with God. God will answer.

Matthew 7

Try knocking on something continuously. The door symbol is a reminder that God is always there to talk and listen to through prayer.

Love

Symbol: heart

Jesus told his followers that it was not enough just to love those who love them. He wanted them to love their enemies, too. Jesus said to do good and pray for those who hate them. He told them to treat others how they would like to be treated. Jesus gave a new command, "Love each other. You must love each other as I have loved you. All people will know that you are my followers if you love each other."

Matthew 5, Luke 7, John 13

The heart symbol is a reminder to show kindness to those who have been unkind, and to think about places in the world that need peace and love.

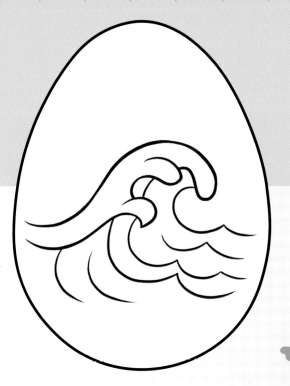

"Be still"

Symbol: wave

Jesus and his friends were sailing across Lake Galilee. Jesus slept. A huge storm arose. The strong wind and the rocky waves tossed the boat around. Jesus' friends panicked and woke Jesus, as they were very afraid that they might drown. With God's power, Jesus spoke to the wind and waves, "Peace. Be still!" and there was complete calm. His friends were amazed. Jesus told them not to be afraid, but to trust him.

Matthew 8, Mark 4, Luke 8

**Is there something that you fear?
The wave symbol is a reminder
to trust God when you are afraid.**

Day 11

Jairus' daughter

Symbol: sleeping

A man named Jairus came to Jesus to beg him to come to his house, for his daughter was dying. When they arrived at the house, Jairus was told his daughter was dead. Jesus told him not to worry but to believe and trust in him, for she was just sleeping. Jesus held the girl's hand and said, "Child, get up!" She awoke from death and was given something to eat. Her parents were astonished.

Matthew 9, Mark 5, Luke 8

Is there someone you know who is ill? Visit them if you can. The sleeping symbol is a reminder that God cares and comforts.

The sower

Symbol: seedling

Jesus compared his work to that of a sower, scattering seed. The seeds are his words about following God. Some of the seeds land on the path, where birds eat them. His words are not heard. On rocky ground, the seedlings are unable to grow strong roots. His words are heard, but given up. Among thorns, the plants are choked. His words are heard, but are given up when things get tough. The good soil produces the best and healthiest plants. These followers base their lives on God's word and their faith grows well.

**Matthew 13,
Mark 4, Luke 8**

Sow a pumpkin seed, look after it as it grows, and watch it flower and produce a pumpkin to harvest later in the year. This is a reminder of how God's word grows inside people.

At the well

Symbol: well

Jesus journeyed through the area of Samaria. He was tired and sat beside a well. There was a woman drawing water. She was alone, as she was ashamed of the bad things she had done in her life. Jesus asked her for a drink. She was surprised, as Jewish people did not like the ways of the Samaritans. Jesus said he offered living water. He had come to give life to everyone. With Jesus in her life, she could change and live well. She rushed off excited to tell others.

John 4

Imagine a life without clean water. Think of those who do not have easy access to water.

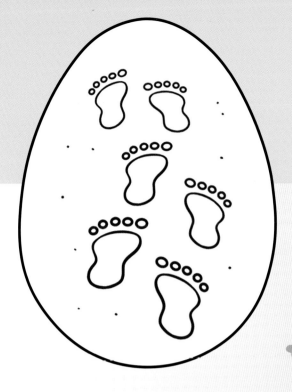

Jesus sent out seventy of his followers to go to every town and place ahead of him. If they were welcomed into homes, he told them to always enter saying, "Peace to this house!" They should stay to eat and drink. If they were not welcomed, then they should move on. In every place, he told them to tell everyone that God's kingdom has come near.

Matthew 10, Mark 6, Luke 10

Do you have a best story about Jesus that you could share with someone? The footprints symbol is a reminder of all those who tell others about Jesus.

Day 15

Martha and Mary

Symbol: ear

When Jesus came to the village of Bethany, a woman named Martha welcomed him into her home. She had a sister named Mary, who sat at Jesus' feet and listened to him speak. Meanwhile, Martha prepared the food and was distracted with other jobs around the house. She complained to Jesus that Mary should be helping her, but Jesus told her that Mary was doing the right thing.

Luke 10

The ear symbol is a reminder to spend time resting in God's presence and of the importance of listening to others.

The Lord's Prayer

Symbol: praying hands

Jesus' followers asked him to teach them how to pray. Jesus told them to speak to God as their Father in heaven. Begin by praising God's name. Pray for God's kingdom to come and that his will be done on earth as in heaven. Ask that God provides for our daily needs and that he forgives our wrongdoings, and in response we forgive others who have wronged us. Ask to be saved from the temptation to not follow God's ways.

The words of the Lord's Prayer can be found in Matthew 6 or Luke 11

The praying hands symbol is a reminder to praise, give thanks, and ask for guidance through prayer. You could write or decorate a prayer.

23

Day 17 Do not worry

Symbol: flying birds

Jesus told his followers that they do not need to worry about whether they will have enough to eat and wear in the future. Instead, they should focus on being part of God's kingdom and these things will be given to them. Jesus said, "Look at the birds: for they do not work to grow food, but God provides for them. The flowers of the fields do not toil, but God clothes them. God values and provides for his children so much more."

Matthew 6, Luke 12

The flying birds symbol is a reminder to not worry about tomorrow. You may want to write down a worry and then throw it away.

The rich fool

Symbol: barn

Jesus told stories called parables to explain his teachings. Jesus was asked to judge an argument between brothers about possessions, but he warned them about being greedy and wanting more than they need. He told them a story about a rich man, who planned to build bigger barns to store his crops, so that he would have enough for the future. But that night he would die, and all that preparation for his future would be for nothing.

Luke 12

The barn symbol is a reminder not to collect lots of possessions, but instead be rich in love, kindness, sharing, and giving things to others.

The mustard seed

Symbol: bird in nest

Jesus told his followers many parables (stories with a deeper meaning) about the kingdom of God. He compared the kingdom to a mustard seed, which is the tiniest of seeds. However, it grows into a great shrub, where birds can nest in its branches.

Matthew 13, Mark 4, Luke 13

The nesting bird symbol is a reminder that even from small beginnings in people's hearts and minds, the smallest of loving actions through faith (trust) in Jesus can make a big difference to others and can grow into something much bigger.

Feeding 5,000

Symbol: basket of bread

A large crowd followed Jesus wherever he went, as the people were eager to hear his words and see him healing the sick. The sun was setting, but the people had not eaten. Rather than send them home, Jesus told his disciples to feed them. Andrew brought to Jesus a young boy, who had two fish and five loaves. Jesus asked his disciples to make the people sit down. There were about five thousand. Then he gave thanks to God for the food and it was passed around. There was enough food to satisfy everyone, and twelve baskets of pieces left over.

Matthew 14, Mark 6, Luke 9, John 6

Think of others without enough food. The basket of bread symbol is a reminder of God's power shown through sharing and giving food to others in need.

Walking on water

Symbol: feet on water

Jesus went into the mountains to pray, while his disciples sailed across the lake. Early in the morning, Jesus came toward them walking on the water. When the disciples saw him, they were afraid, thinking that he was a ghost. Jesus told them not to be afraid. Peter trusted Jesus and climbed out of the boat and started walking toward him. Then he felt the strong wind and began to sink, crying out, "Lord, save me!" Straightaway Jesus reached out his hand to catch Peter, asking, "Why did you doubt?" The wind stopped as they climbed into the boat. The disciples praised Jesus as the Son of God.

Matthew 14, Mark 6, John 6

The symbol of the feet on water is a reminder to keep focused on Jesus and his words for support. Does a friend need encouragement?

Dazzling figures

Symbol: mountain

Jesus led his disciples, Peter, James, and John, up a high mountain away from everyone else. Suddenly Jesus' appearance changed before them. His face glowed and his clothes became dazzling white. The ancient prophets Elijah and Moses appeared, talking with Jesus. The disciples were terrified. Then a cloud covered the sight, and a voice came from the cloud, saying, "This is my own dear Son. Listen to him!" Afterwards, Jesus told them not to tell anyone what they had seen until he had risen from death.

Matthew 17, Mark 9, Luke 9

Like the wonder seen by the disciples on the mountain, think about something wonderful that has happened.

The good Samaritan

Symbol: donkey

Jesus was asked how to receive eternal life. He told this story about a Jewish man who was on his way from the city of Jerusalem to Jericho. The man was attacked, robbed, and left injured on the road. A Jewish priest and then a Levite from the temple walked past, but both crossed over to avoid the man. A Samaritan also came along the road. He stopped, wrapped the man's wounds, and helped the man onto his donkey. He took the injured man to an inn and paid for his care. Jesus said, "Go and do the same, to show love for others."

Luke 10

As a donkey carries others, so think about charities that provide support for those in need.

The banquet

Symbol: balloon

Jesus told a story about who is invited into God's kingdom. A king was giving a great banquet for his son. When it was ready, a servant was sent out to call those who had been invited, but they were too busy to come. So the king sent out his servants to invite everyone in the streets, both good and bad, the poor and the sick. The hall was filled with guests, but one was not wearing the right clothes, so he was taken away.

Matthew 22, Luke 14

The balloon symbol is a reminder of the great celebration of the new kingdom of heaven and earth that God has planned.

The lost sheep

Symbol: sheep

The religious leaders were grumbling that Jesus ate with those who had done wrong. Jesus told them this parable about a shepherd who had one hundred sheep. One day, he found that one was lost, so he left the flock and went in search of it. He searched until he found the lost sheep and then carried it home on his shoulders. He called together his friends and celebrated that he had found his missing sheep. Jesus said there was joy in heaven when someone who had done wrong says sorry and turns back to God's way.

Matthew 18, Luke 15

The lost sheep symbol is a reminder of God's joy when someone turns back to follow Jesus. Is there someone that you have lost contact with?

The lost son

Symbol: pigs

Jesus told this parable about God's love and forgiveness. There was a man who had two sons. The younger son asked his father for his share of the property. Once he was given the money, he left home. In a distant country, the younger son spent all the money, recklessly. He then had to take the lowest of jobs, feeding pigs. He realized that even his father's workers did not go hungry, so he set off for home. While he was still a long way off, his father saw him and ran to hug him. The son said sorry, but his father clothed him and celebrated. The older son was annoyed, but his father explained that his brother had been lost but was now found.

Matthew 21, Luke 15

Like the younger son feeding the pigs, who lost his way, there are times when we do wrong to others and to God and need to say sorry.

33

Thank you

Symbol: Number 10

10

On the way to Jerusalem, Jesus entered a village where ten people with a skin disease called out for his help. Jesus told them to go and show themselves to the priests, and as they went, their skin disease disappeared. One of them turned back, praising God, and thanked Jesus for healing him. Jesus asked where the other nine were and was saddened that only one had returned.

Luke 17

10

The number ten symbol is a reminder to be thankful to God and to others who have shown kindness.

The children

Symbol: smiley face

Among the large crowds surrounding Jesus were people bringing their babies and young children for him to bless. Jesus' disciples thought that Jesus was too busy and turned them away. But Jesus saw this and told them not to stop the little children from coming, for the kingdom of God belongs to those who receive it as a little child. Jesus took the children in his arms and blessed them.

Matthew 19, Mark 10

Imagine Jesus holding you in his arms. The smiley face symbol is a reminder that Jesus loves children and thinks they set an example to adults for simply loving and trusting God.

Bartimaeus

Symbol: dark glasses

There was a man named Bartimaeus sitting on the roadside outside the city of Jericho. He could not see, so he could only beg for help from passers-by. When he heard that Jesus was walking past, Bartimaeus called out for help. Jesus stopped and Bartimaeus asked to be able to see again. Jesus replied that his belief had healed him. At once Bartimaeus could see again, and he followed Jesus.

Mark 10

Can you imagine not being able to see? Think of those who are not able to do certain things, and of their carers.

Zacchaeus

Symbol: money bag

In the city of Jericho, there was a tax collector named Zacchaeus, who had become rich by taking more money than he should have. When Jesus came to Jericho, Zacchaeus tried to see him, but Zacchaeus was a short man and could not see above the crowd. He ran ahead and climbed a sycamore tree for a better view. As Jesus passed under the tree, he looked up and told Zacchaeus to come down, as he was going to stay with him. The crowd grumbled, but Zacchaeus changed after speaking with Jesus. He gave to the poor and paid back four times the amount he had taken.

Luke 19

The money bag symbol is a reminder to avoid a love of money, and to give to those in need.

Day 31 The talents

Symbol: rosette

Jesus knew that he would soon be going away, so he encouraged his disciples to use their talents. He told them a parable about a man who, before going on a journey, summoned his servants and gave one five thousand coins, another two thousand coins, and another one thousand coins. The first servant traded his coins and made ten thousand. The second servant did the same and made two thousand more. The third servant dug a hole to keep his coins hidden. When the man returned, he was impressed with the first two servants and rewarded them, but the third servant was thrown out.

Matthew 25, Luke 19

The rosette symbol is a reminder that gifts are from God to be used for his glory. Think about your gifts and how best they could be used to help others.

Lazarus

Symbol: teardrops

Martha and Mary had a brother named Lazarus, who was dying. They sent a message to Jesus to come but he delayed. Lazarus died. His body was wrapped in burial cloths and laid in a tomb. Four days later, Jesus came and wept with Martha and Mary. Then he went to the tomb and asked for the stone in front of it to be removed. After thanking God for listening, he cried with a loud voice, "Lazarus, come out!" The dead man came out and they unbound him. The people who saw this believed that Jesus was God's promised king. The news spread.

John 11

> **The teardrop symbol is a reminder that God provides comfort to those who mourn and are sad. Think of those who give comfort to others.**

Day 33

The true vine

Symbol: grapes

Grapevines were grown throughout the area where Jesus lived. He described himself as the true vine, the trunk where the roots grow deep. Jesus told his followers to abide in, or hold on to, him. The branches can only grow fruit if they are connected to the trunk. The branches are pruned to bear more fruit that glorifies God.

John 15

The grapes symbol is a reminder for followers of Jesus to remain in his love and care so that they will live fruitful lives.

Entering Jerusalem

Symbol: palm branch

The Jewish festival of Passover was soon, and many people were making their way to the city of Jerusalem. As Jesus came near the city, he asked two disciples to fetch a young donkey. Jesus rode the colt along the road to Jerusalem. People recognized him and spread their coats along the road and cut palm branches from the trees to lay before him. They went ahead of him shouting and praising him as God's promised king.

Matthew 21, Mark 11, Luke 19, John 12

The palm branch symbol is a reminder of the joyful Palm Sunday celebration, praising Jesus as God's promised king, who has come to save the world.

Washing feet

Symbol: bowl and towel

Jesus and his disciples met in an upper room to celebrate the Passover meal. Jesus knew this was his last supper. During the meal, he got up, tied a towel around himself, and poured water into a bowl. He then began to wash his disciples' feet and wipe them with the towel. Afterwards he told his disciples that he had set them an example to serve one another as he had served them.

John 13

The symbol of the bowl and towel is a reminder that Jesus' followers are humble and serve others. Think of those who serve others and help you.

The last supper

Symbol: cup

Jesus sat down with his disciples for the Passover meal. He told them that he would not eat again until he had fulfilled God's plan. He took some bread, gave thanks, broke it, and shared it with them, saying, "This bread is my body that I am giving for you. Do this to remember me." After supper, he also took a cup, gave thanks, and passed it around, saying, "This cup shows the new agreement that God makes with his people. This new agreement begins with my blood, which is poured out for you." Jesus then said one of them would betray him. Judas left the room.

**Matthew 26, Mark 14,
Luke 22**

Remember the good times that you have spent with others. Jesus wanted his friends to remember him through the sharing of bread and the cup.

The garden

Symbol: olive tree

After supper, Jesus went to pray in a garden of olive trees on the hillside outside Jerusalem. His disciples went with him, and Jesus asked them to pray with him, but they fell asleep. Jesus prayed, "Father, if you will, take this cup of suffering away from me. Not my will, however, but your will be done." As he prayed for strength, the noise of a crowd was heard. Judas led them and came forward to kiss Jesus. The temple guard arrested him.

Matthew 26, Mark 14, Luke 22, John 17

The olive tree symbol is a reminder of how Jesus talked to God about suffering. Think about someone who is sad and having a difficult time.

Peter's betrayal

Symbol: cockerel

At the last supper, Jesus had said that all his friends would desert him. Peter said that he would not. After the arrest, Peter followed Jesus to the house of the chief priest at a distance. He slipped into the courtyard. One of the servants recognized him as being with Jesus, but Peter denied knowing him. A second time he was asked, and then a third time. Each time Peter declared he did not know Jesus. Then the cock crowed, and Peter remembered Jesus' words and wept.

Matthew 26, Mark 14, Luke 22, John 18

Have you ever defended a friend? The cockerel symbol is a reminder of the courage needed to stand strong to do the right thing.

45

Crucified

Symbol: cross

Jesus was tried before the Jewish council and accused of claiming to be God. They handed him over to the Roman governor, Pontius Pilate, to be sentenced, but he did not think Jesus had done anything wrong. The chief priests and elders stirred up the crowd, who shouted for Jesus to be crucified like a criminal. Pilate washed his hands and sentenced Jesus to death on a cross. The soldiers mocked Jesus and placed a crown of thorns on his head. The sign nailed on the cross above Jesus' head read "The King of the Jews". As Jesus died, darkness covered the land.

Matthew 27, Mark 15, Luke 23, John 19

What does the symbol of the cross mean to you?

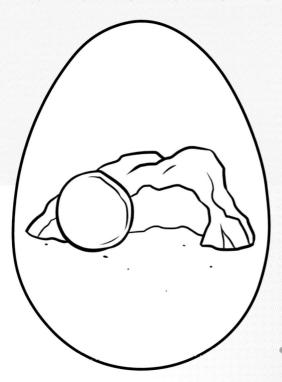

Raised

Symbol: empty tomb

Jesus' body was laid in a tomb and a stone rolled across the entrance. Early in the morning, after the day of rest, the women who loved Jesus went to his tomb with burial spices. There was a strong earthquake and a figure in dazzling white rolled the stone away. The angel told them, "Jesus is not here. He has risen from death as he said he would." The tomb was empty. They rushed to tell Jesus' followers. Suddenly, Jesus met them, saying, "Greetings!" The women fell at his feet and praised him.

**Matthew 28, Mark 16,
Luke 24, John 20**

The empty tomb symbol is a reminder of Jesus triumphing over the sins of the world and death. Enjoy celebrating Easter!

**You can read more about these stories about
Jesus in a children's Bible from Lion Hudson:**

The Lion Easy-Read Bible

The Lion Bible to Keep For Ever

The Lion Wondrous Bible

The Lion Children's Bible

The Children's Bible in 365 Stories

The Lion Day-by-Day Bible